Consumer Attitudes Toward Data Breach Notifications and Loss of Personal Information

Lillian Ablon, Paul Heaton, Diana Catherine Lavery,
Sasha Romanosky

For more information on this publication, visit www.rand.org/t/rr1187

Library of Congress Cataloging-in-Publication Data is available for this publication.
ISBN: 978-0-8330-9312-7

Published by the RAND Corporation, Santa Monica, Calif.

© Copyright 2016 RAND Corporation

RAND® is a registered trademark.

Cover: Image via pathdoc/Fotolia

Support RAND

Make a tax-deductible charitable contribution at
www.rand.org/giving/contribute

www.rand.org

Preface

Data breaches continue to plague private-sector companies, nonprofit organizations, and government agencies. Although spending on cybersecurity continues to grow, companies are still being breached, and sensitive personal, financial, and health information is still being compromised. As of March 2016, 47 states and the District of Columbia have adopted laws that require companies to notify individuals in the event that their personal information is lost or stolen. This report sets out the results of a study of consumer attitudes toward data breaches, notifications that a breach has occurred, and company responses to such events.

The report should provide valuable information that can be used by businesses and policymakers as they develop policies and best practices related to information security and data breach response. Moreover, it should be of interest to individuals who conduct business with any organization that holds their personal and confidential data.

RAND Institute for Civil Justice

The RAND Institute for Civil Justice (ICJ) is dedicated to improving the civil justice system by supplying policymakers and the public with rigorous and nonpartisan research. Its studies identify trends in litigation and inform policy choices about liability, compensation, regulation, risk management, and insurance. The institute builds on a long tradition of RAND Corporation research characterized by an interdisciplinary, empirical approach to public policy issues and rigorous standards of quality, objectivity, and independence.

ICJ research is supported by pooled grants from a range of sources, including corporations, trade and professional associations, individuals, government agencies, and private foundations. All its reports are subject to peer review and disseminated widely to policymakers, practitioners in law and business, other researchers, and the public.

The ICJ is part of RAND Justice, Infrastructure, and Environment, a division of the RAND Corporation dedicated to improving policy- and decisionmaking in a wide range of policy domains, including civil and criminal justice, infrastructure protection and homeland security, transportation and energy policy, and environmental and natural resource policy.

Questions or comments about this report should be sent to the project leader, Lillian Ablon (Lillian_Ablon@rand.org). For more information about the RAND Institute for Civil Justice, see www.rand.org/icj or contact the director at icjdirector@rand.org.

Contents

Figures and Tables

Summary

Data breaches continue to plague private-sector companies, nonprofit organizations, and government agencies. Target, Home Depot, the Office of Personnel and Management, Anthem, JPMorgan Chase, and thousands of other organizations have suffered breaches of sensitive personal, financial, and health information, affecting hundreds of millions of individuals.

As of March 2016, 47 states have passed legislation requiring companies to notify individuals when a breach occurs. The purpose of this requirement is to give consumers the chance to respond quickly to protect themselves from further harm and to shine a light on the breached company. As Justice Louis D. Brandeis famously said, "Publicity is justly commended as a remedy for social and industrial diseases. Sunlight is said to be the best of disinfectants" (Brandeis, 1914, p. 92). Public notification of a breach, therefore, highlights the weaknesses of a company's data security practices and can create an incentive for the company to avoid such risk in the future.

Despite the mounting rate of security breaches, the continuing harms imposed on consumers and firms, and more than a decade of breach-notification laws, very little research exists that examines consumer response to these developments.[1] To address this gap, this research launched a first-of-its-kind consumer survey designed to provide useful information to companies, policymakers, and the public about the consumer's experience of data loss.

---

[1] Other studies have examined firm behavior, firm responses, and firm costs resulting from data breaches.

While there are several potential research questions regarding consumer sentiment toward data breach and notifications,[2] this survey was intended to examine the following: the frequency of breach notifications and types of data lost; consumer response toward the notification, company, and the company's follow-on actions after a breach; and perceived personal costs resulting from a breach.

The survey was conducted using the American Life Panel, a nationally representative panel of more than 6,000 adults who participate in Internet-based surveys covering a diverse set of issues. Fielded between May 15 and June 1, 2015, the survey was designed to provide a snapshot of the frequency of breach notifications and the types of data compromised, as well as consumer reactions to the breach, the notification process, and the affected company. The survey also examined estimates regarding the personal cost of the breach, as well as suggestions regarding future notifications and data protection measures. The data gathered and analyzed from this survey come from participant self-report and recall. As such, the data may be incomplete due to limits of memory, underreported due to forgetfulness of past notifications, or overreported due to increased media reporting (e.g., hearing about a data breach and misremembering being a part of it).

Survey Results

Twenty-six percent of respondents, or an estimated 64 million adults in the United States, recalled receiving a breach notification in the 12-month period before the survey.

While 44 percent of those surveyed had received a notification of their information being part of data breach sometime in their lives,

---

[2] For example, other research questions can include the following: Is the breach notice effective as a risk communication (i.e., Do consumers understand or notice a data breach notice? Do consumers have any choices about data breach? Does the notice communicate what the choices are?)? Does the breach notice change user behavior (i.e., Do users make economic decisions based on the breach notice, such as changing where they shop, but still buying the same goods? Do consumers opt out of certain markets due to concerns from the breach?)?

26 percent of our respondents recalled receiving one or more notifications within the year prior to the survey (June 2014 to June 2015). We therefore estimate that more than one-quarter of all U.S. adults, or 64 million people, received a notification of compromised personal information in that year. Higher-income and better-educated respondents were more likely to remember experiencing a breach, and younger adults (ages 18–34) and senior citizens (ages 65+) were less likely. Further, more than one-half of those people (51 percent), or an estimated 36 million individuals, received two or more notifications in the year preceding the survey.

Of those who received a notification in their lifetime, 44 percent were already aware of the breach.

Of those participants who remembered receiving a data breach notification over their lifetime, most (56 percent) first learned of the breach from the company notification. However, 44 percent initially learned about the breach from a source other than the affected company, typically from media reports or from a third party, such as a bank. Just 10 percent discovered the breach by identifying suspicious activity.

Sixty-two percent of respondents accepted offers of free credit monitoring.

Despite evidence suggesting otherwise, an overwhelming 62 percent of respondents reported having accepted offers of free credit monitoring. According to respondents, three main factors influenced their decision: (1) time and effort required, (2) quality perception and trust (both of the affected company and of the breach-notification service), and (3) whether the offer duplicated other services the victim had.

Only 11 percent of respondents stopped dealing with the company following a breach.

Most respondents (89 percent) continued to conduct business with the breached firm, while only 11 percent stopped conducting business with it. One percent reported increasing the amount of business they conduct with the breached firm.

Of those who estimated a dollar value–equivalent cost of the breach and any inconvenience it garnered, the median cost was $500.

Thirty-two percent of respondents felt that the breach imposed no dollar loss to them. Of the remaining 68 percent who estimated some financial loss from the breach, the median loss was $500. Median dollar values were higher if health information ($1,000), Social Security numbers ($1,000), or other financial information ($864) was compromised. Further, just under 6 percent said that the inconvenience cost them $10,000 or more. Of those who experienced an extreme inconvenience, the breach typically involved credit card or health information.

Seventy-seven percent of respondents were highly satisfied with the company's post-breach response.

Attitudes toward the breached company were found to be very favorable. Most respondents (77 percent) were highly satisfied with the company's breach response. The greatest difference was with ethnic minorities,[3] who were less likely to be satisfied with the company's breach response and more likely to both place a higher dollar value on the inconvenience caused by the breach and cease doing business with the company.

Respondents recommended several steps companies could take to better protect their data.

The survey asked participants to identify actions they would recommend and actions they would discourage on the part of companies after a data breach. The steps that would highly satisfy most respondents were (1) take measures to ensure that a similar breach cannot occur in the future (68 percent), (2) offer free credit monitoring or similar services to ensure that lost data are not misused (64 percent), and (3) notify consumers immediately (63 percent). All three of these actions were valued more highly than receiving financial compensation for the inconvenience. The steps with which respondents were least

---

[3] In other words, those who classified themselves as Hispanic/Latino, non-Hispanic black, or non-Hispanic other.

satisfied were donating money to organizations that promote cybersecurity and simply apologizing to those affected.

Implications

We anticipate that these results will help establish a baseline understanding regarding consumer attitudes toward data loss and firm responses. They also have implications for business practices, regulatory policy, and the public. For example, companies can take note of preferred ways to respond to customers and adjust other business practices; policymakers and regulatory agencies can review notification methods and data breach laws to speed up notification and prevent further harm with any stolen data.

More than one-quarter of respondents remember receiving a data breach notification in the 12 months preceding the survey, and more than one-half of those respondents remember receiving two or more. This may be indicative of a world increasingly dependent on digital components. That 44 percent of consumers were already aware of a breach before receiving a notification from the company may be a result of the role that media reports, banks, credit monitoring, and other third-party services play in informing consumers of a data breach. Knowing that many consumers have this awareness may help companies revise their timing and strategies for disclosing a breach to both consumers and the public. Contrary to past data and studies, 62 percent of respondents reported accepting offers of free credit monitoring, up from a reported 10–29 percent. This suggests that consumers may feel that recent breaches or recent data loss warrants protection—whether they suffer from "breach fatigue" or not. Most respondents (77 percent) were highly satisfied with the company's breach response, and only a few (11 percent) stopped doing business with the firm, suggesting that consumers appear to feel that companies are responding appropriately to the consequences of a data breach. This may or may not induce companies to change or improve breach-notification practices.

Acknowledgments

RAND reports typically draw on a wide collection of supporters, collaborators, and helpers in their creation. We would first like to thank the RAND Institute for Civil Justice for its generous support to make this research possible. Our reviewers, Deirdre Mulligan, professor at the University of California, Berkeley School of Information, and Rebecca Balebako, information scientist at the RAND Corporation, offered sage feedback and suggestions that improved the report. Laura Zakaras gave generously of her time to help with the flow and format. Cameron Wright, Matt Baird, and Diana Naranjo provided exceptional additional statistical analysis.

CHAPTER ONE

Introduction

Data breaches have become commonplace in the United States, and can be the result of malicious, unintentional, or accidental events. Malicious causes include hacking computer systems (either by employees or by external individuals or groups); theft of laptops, portable memory devices, or other physical hardware; and social engineering techniques of deception or misrepresentation. Unintentional or accidental causes include loss of laptops, portable memory devices, or other physical hardware; unintentional exposure on unsecured websites; and improper disposal of data, such as improperly shredding personal documents or disposing of personal records in a dumpster. Once a breach occurs, personal data can appear within days on black markets, enabling criminals to sell financial, health, and identity information (Ablon, Libicki, and Golay, 2014; Cárdenas et al., 2009) and causing various forms of identity, tax, and loan fraud (Herr and Romanosky, 2015). The victims of identity theft experience a wide range of costs—both financial and inconvenience-based—in efforts to repair their damaged credit records and prevent further harm (Romanosky and Acquisti, 2009; Government Accountability Office, 2007).

The Bureau of Justice Statistics estimates that 17.6 million people were victims of identity theft in 2014 (Harrell, 2015; up from 16.6 million people in 2012 [Harrell and Langton, 2013]) and, based on a 2003 survey on identity theft conducted by the Federal Trade Commission, most victims are women, people with higher incomes, and people with higher levels of education (Anderson, 2005).

It is not surprising that data breaches across all sectors—health (e.g., Anthem Blue Cross), retail (e.g., Target), finance (e.g., JPMorgan Chase), and government (e.g., the Office of Personnel and Management)—have lowered the public's confidence in the protection of their personal data by these organizations and agencies. A recent Pew Research Center study found that only 6 percent of adults were "very confident" that government agencies could keep their records secure, and just 9 percent were "very confident" that credit card companies can keep their records secure (Madden and Rainie, 2015). Email providers, telephone companies, online search engines, and social media sites were the least trusted (Madden and Rainie, 2015).

A data breach also imposes many costs on the organization suffering the breach. For example, the organization must investigate the cause of the breach; repair and restore any information technology systems; notify consumers; establish consumer call centers; and pay any legal fees, settlement awards, and credit monitoring (Romanosky, Telang, and Acquisti, 2011).

In response to these breaches and their resulting costs, most states now require companies to notify individuals in the case of the loss or theft of personally identifiable information.[1] As of March 2016, 47 states, the District of Columbia, Guam, Puerto Rico, and the Virgin Islands have such laws.[2] Efforts for federal legislation have stalled, and the only three states that have yet to implement a data security breach-notification law are Alabama, New Mexico, and South Dakota (see National Conference of State Legislatures, 2016).

Despite slight variation across state legislation, these laws are intended to have two effects: first, to empower consumers to take action

---

[1] *Personally identifiable information* is generally such information as Social Security numbers, driver's license numbers, credit card numbers, or medical information. Some states (California, for example) do not require a disclosure if data other than these were compromised or lost (usernames and passwords, for example) (Hoofnagle and King, 2008).

[2] Some commentators believe that the European Commission's General Data Protection Regulation is likely to include a general security breach-notification requirement for data controllers. Currently, there is a European Union (EU)–wide requirement for telecoms, and particular EU member states have adopted them in various sectors. As such, this research may also be useful in the EU General Data Protection Regulation process.

to mitigate any potential harm caused by the breach, and, second, to force companies to bear more of the cost of their risky actions and induce them to increase their investment in data-protection controls. As Justice Louis D. Brandeis famously said, "Publicity is justly commended as a remedy for social and industrial diseases. Sunlight is said to be the best of disinfectants" (Brandeis, 1914, p. 92). Public notification of a data breach, therefore, sheds light on the weaknesses of a company's data security practices and can create an incentive for the company to avoid such risk in the future.

The Purpose of This Study

Despite the mounting rate of security breaches, the continuing harms imposed on consumers and firms, and many years of breach-notification laws, very little research exists that examines the consumer's response to these developments. Although many studies have examined firm behavior, firm responses, and firm costs resulting from data breaches (see, for example, Ponemon Institute, 2015; NetDiligence, 2014; Shey, 2015), few studies have examined the consumer perspective (e.g., Ponemon Institute, 2014). To address this gap, the RAND Corporation initiated a first-of-its-kind consumer survey designed to provide useful information to consumers and policymakers about consumers' experiences of data loss and their attitudes toward companies responsible for that loss.

This survey, which used the American Life Panel to reach a representative sample of American adults, was designed to provide a snapshot of the frequency of notifications of data breaches; the types of data breached; and individual sentiment toward the notification, the company, and its follow-on actions after the breach. The survey also examined perceived personal costs resulting from the breach, individuals' suggestions for future notifications, actions companies might take to improve data protection, and respondent comfort with computing technology. We note that the data gathered and analyzed from this survey come from participant self-report and recall. As such, the data may be incomplete due to limits of memory, underreported due to forgetfulness of past notifications, or overreported due to increased media reporting (e.g., hearing about a data breach and misremembering being a part of it). With that caveat, these results can help establish a baseline of information about consumer attitudes toward data loss and will have implications for company practices in responding to such events.

The Survey

The American Life Panel

The data used in this analysis were generated from the RAND American Life Panel, a nationally representative panel of more than 6,000 members ages 18 and older who have agreed to participate in occasional Internet-based surveys.[3] In contrast to many large-scale data efforts that focus on single topics, the American Life Panel is used by researchers to address a wide range of important policy issues concerning the social and economic status of the American population. Because the panel allows surveys to be fielded so quickly, the results can provide a "real-time pulse" of the public on changing conditions in contemporary American life. Since its inception in 2006, more than 400 surveys have been fielded in the United States and around the world to address such topics as spending and savings at the height of the Great Recession, opinions about the rollout of the Patient Protection and Affordable Care Act, beliefs and decisions about flu vaccinations, joint retirement decisions, and predictions regarding presidential elections.

Survey Characteristics

Our survey was fielded between May 14 and June 1, 2015, to 2,618 adults.[4] Of those, 2,038 individuals completed the survey, for a

---

[3] The American Life Panel exploits a probability-based design, which implies that the sample of respondents is derived from a larger population of individuals, as opposed to a school- or clinic-based sample, in which the full population of potential candidates is known.

[4] Note that our survey was conducted before the data breach at the U.S. Office of Management and Budget, which was disclosed in June 2015. As a result, consumer sentiment may have changed since the event.

response rate of 78 percent.[5] (For details about the demographics of the respondents, see Appendix B.) In the analysis that follows, we applied survey weights to our sample to ensure that the respondents were representative of the U.S. adult population in terms of gender, age, race/ethnicity, education, and income (see RAND American Life Panel, undated).

Survey Limitations

As with all surveys, ours is not without limitations. For example, it is possible that respondents inaccurately recall their experiences with data breaches. Studies of consumer memory have shown more-accurate recall for recent events than for events in the more-distant past (Groves, 1989). Because it may be harder to recall experiences in the distant past, we attempt to mitigate recall bias by asking respondents about their *most-recent* experience with lost data for the bulk of our analysis. Our results suggest that most respondents who have lost personal information have had such an experience within the past 12 months. While not a panacea, by focusing only on the most-recent experience, the majority of which has been in the past 12 months, we attempt to attenuate recall problems.

A number of the survey questions were subjective, including the request that respondents assign a dollar value to the hassle and disutility they experienced when dealing with the data breach, as well as questions concerning any suggested remedies to companies following a breach. We made no effort to anchor the cost question, and a small number of respondents reported costs that were implausibly large. In considering remedies, respondents may inaccurately forecast the types of remedies they may actually prefer, or they might not provide truthful answers. However, we saw no reason to expect particular problems with these questions beyond the usual limitations inherent in subjective survey questions.

---

[5]   The average time for participants to complete the survey was 3.4 minutes. Three individuals did not provide an end time (i.e., they dropped out of the survey without completing it). Participants are paid a rate of $40 per hour for answering surveys, prorated down to the approximate length of the survey. This particular survey paid $3 for completing it.

Further, because ours is an Internet-based survey, it may target a population that differs from the general adult population in terms of their facility with information and communication technologies or technology usage habits. That said, American Life Panel participants are initially recruited onto the panel using a variety of methods, and anyone without Internet access is offered a laptop and an Internet subscription. In other words, the recruitment process is specifically designed to include people who may not themselves be Internet users. To the extent that respondents are unrepresentative of the population in terms of technology use, they are likely to be skewed toward people who are heavier users—an important group in terms of knowledge of data breaches.

Finally, despite prevalence of notification requirements, not all breaches are publicly reported. Privacy Rights Clearinghouse, Identity Theft Resource Center, and Advisen are three organizations that track data breaches reported in newspapers, magazines, and other news outlets. The website informationisbeautiful.com also provides an appealing visualization of some of the largest data breaches.[6] Despite these data sources, analysis of three separate data sets by the Government Accountability Office from January 2005 to January 2006 identified sufficient differences, suggesting that, together, they likely understate the true extent of data breaches (Government Accountability Office, 2007). This underreporting effect may exist for a number of reasons: (1) a company may not be aware that it has suffered a data breach;[7] (2) even if the company *is* aware, it is not always required to notify the public;[8] and (3) companies tend to not want to disclose that they have

---

[6]   See "World's Biggest Data Breaches," undated.

[7]   Verizon's *2014 Data Breach Investigations Report* found that 70–80 percent of breaches are discovered by third parties, rather than the affected company. See Verizon, 2014.

[8]   For example, some state laws provide exemptions for small breaches (fewer than 500 records stolen), in which the compromised information was encrypted, or for which there is already a sector-specific notification requirement (e.g., Health Insurance Portability and Accountability Act, Gramm-Leach-Bliley Act).

been victims of a data breach—either for reputational reasons (Libicki, Ablon, and Webb, 2015) or for forensic purposes.[9]

Next, we present our survey results, followed by discussion and implications for business, consumers, and policymakers.

---

[9] For example, a company may still be under attack and trying to "root out" the attacker and might not want to alert the attacker that it is aware of the breach.

CHAPTER TWO

Survey Results

In this chapter, we provide the results to our survey questions. Specifically, we examined the frequency with which respondents had received breach notifications, how they came to learn of the breach, and the kinds of information that were compromised. We also examined consumer responses to the breach by asking respondents about offers of credit monitoring or other post-breach assistance, customer loyalty, and other post-breach actions they may have taken. Finally, we examine self-reported estimates of financial loss and overall satisfaction with firm responses following the breach.

Frequency of Data Breach Notifications

Respondents were asked whether they had ever been notified by a company that their personal information had been stolen due to a hack or data breach. Figure 2.1 shows the incidence of recalled breach notifications over a lifetime. Overall, 43 percent of respondents reported receiving a notice—an estimated 105 million Americans.[1]

There are statistically significant demographic differences among those who reported receiving data breach notifications over their lifetimes—by age group, family income, education, and race/ethnic-

---

[1] The survey did not distinguish between different types of notices (e.g., email versus paper notice). The 95-percent confidence interval rests between 99.9 million and 110.5 million, based on the 2014 U.S. adult population of 245.2 million (see U.S. Census Bureau, undated).

Figure 2.1
Percentage of Participants Who Recalled Receiving a Breach Notification in Their Lifetime (n = 2,038)

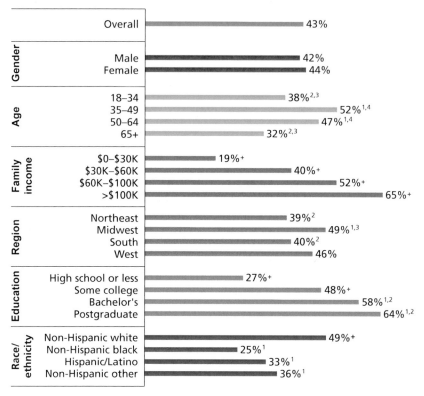

NOTE: + denotes statistically significant differences from all other groups within a demographic category. [1,2,3] or [4] denotes statistically significant differences from the noted group, within a demographic category. For example, within the demographic category "Family Income," every group ($0–$30K, $30K–$60K, $60K–$100K, >$100K) was statistically different from each other; within the demographic category "Region," the results of the second group (Midwest) were significantly different from the first and third groups (Northeast and South, respectively), and the fourth group (West) had no statistical difference from any of the other groups. Significance was calculated at $p < 0.05$ for all noted differences using the Wald test (i.e., one can say with 95-percent confidence that there is a notable difference).

RAND RR1187-2.1

ity (Figure 2.1).[2] For example, non-Hispanic whites were more likely to have received notifications than all other races and ethnicities; there were broad differences in instances of notification across all levels of family income (each was statistically significant from the others); and those with college degrees were significantly more likely to report having received a data breach notification than those without college degrees.

Age: A priori, it is unclear which age group would be expected to be victims of a data breach (and therefore receive more breach notifications). On one hand, older adults (i.e., baby boomers) may be *less likely* to be victims of data breach than younger cohorts (e.g., millennials and members of Generation X), because of lower use of technology (Zickuhr, 2011). On the other hand, older individuals may be *more* vulnerable to loss of information, due to lower sophistication, comfort, or awareness of security risks (Microsoft Corporate Blogs, 2014), as well as more assets (e.g., financial accounts). Our survey response reveals that, although loss of information is a significant problem for all age groups, and those aged 65 or older are less comfortable with technology than the younger generations, having received a notification was less common among the youngest and oldest cohorts than among those aged 35–64.

Family income: The responses reveal a significant gradient by family income, with the wealthiest income group (more than $100,000 in annual income) recalling having received notices at a rate more than triple that of the lowest income group (65 percent versus 19 percent). This may be explained by the notion that those with greater income engage in more financial and recreational activities with more organizations, resulting in an increased risk of compromise of personal information.[3]

Region: There is relatively little variation in the incidence of data breach notifications across regions of the country, although those in the Midwest are modestly more likely to have received breach notifications (49 percent). If it is true that the distribution of breached organizations

---

[2] Wald tests of simple hypotheses were conducted after linear regression of the question responses and the demographic categories of interest in order to determine any differences between the categories. All differences reported herein are significant at the 0.05 level.

[3] While our tests were run to compare at the 0.05 significance level, we found that, for family income, each pairwise difference in proportions was statistically different at the 0.01 significance level.

(including private, nonprofit, and government agencies) is somewhat uniform across regions, this would indeed account for the similarity.

Education: Those with college or postgraduate degrees were more than twice as likely (58 percent and 64 percent, respectively) to report having received data breach notifications as those with high school diplomas or less (27 percent). Education level also reflects relative comfort with modern technology (66 percent and 62 percent for postgraduate and bachelor's degrees, respectively, versus 36 percent for those with high school degrees or less). The variation between education levels could also be explained by age. That is, those with less education may be younger and have had less opportunity to conduct business with as many firms (e.g., mortgage companies, hospitals, credit card companies), resulting in fewer instances of personal information available to firms that may later suffer a breach.

Race/ethnicity: Non-Hispanic whites reported receiving significantly more notifications than all other race/ethnic groups. In particular, they reported receiving twice as many notifications as non-Hispanic blacks (49 percent versus 24 percent).

Location: As mentioned, there are currently three states that have no notification laws: Alabama, New Mexico, and South Dakota. Respondents in these three states had lower rates of having ever received a notice (43 percent) than respondents in states with notification laws (51 percent), although this difference is not statistically significant (t-stat = 1.03).[4] This may not be surprising if most breaches affect individuals in multiple states, and there are many legal and compliance reasons for notifying those whose states do not have laws. It may also be more convenient (and responsible) for a firm to notify all individuals, rather than spending time to omit some individuals from select states.

We postulate that some of these patterns may also be explained by differential *access* to information and communication technologies: In the past, those in the younger cohorts, those in higher income groups, those with college or postgraduate degrees, and non-Hispanic whites have perhaps had more opportunities for interaction with tech-

---

[4] A Wald test did not yield a statistically significant relationship, likely due to the very low sample size from the affected states.

nology (not only with personally owned devices but also interactions with technology in offices, hospitals, hotels, retail stores, etc.), resulting in more opportunities for their information to be compromised. That said, access to technology does not necessarily imply greater probability of receiving a breach notice.

Furthermore, some groups may have more-accurate recall of data breach notifications. For example, those with higher levels of education might be more likely to read and understand a data breach notification and thereby report higher levels of having received a breach notification. Recent (May 2015) proposed legislation in California cites that breach notifications are often written at the college level and recommends changes to notification language to be clearer and easier to understand (Senate Rules Committee, State Senate of California, 2015).

Given that many data breaches occur in the digital realm, another possible explanation could be a victim's *comfort* with modern technology, though our findings do not support this theory (see Table B.1 in Appendix B for responses to comfort with modern technology).

Respondents were also asked whether they had received a data breach notification within the past 12 months.[5] Although 43 percent reported having received at least one data breach notification in their lifetime, 26 percent had received at least one in the year before the survey (i.e., 60 percent of those who have ever received a breach notice), an estimated 64 million individuals.[6] Figure 2.2 provides the breakdown.

We found that notifications were more uniform among those who received a notification in the 12 months before the survey than among those who recalled receiving them in their lifetimes. This may be explained by considering that, in the past year, those of all ages, in all income groups, of all education levels, and of every ethnicity now have better access to information and communication technologies or interact with services and companies that have employed more technol-

---

[5] That is, between June 2014 and June 2015.

[6] The 95-percent confidence interval rests between 59.1 million and 68.4 million, based on the 2014 U.S. adult population of 245.2 million (see U.S. Census Bureau, undated).

Figure 2.2
Percentage of Participants Who Recalled Receiving a Breach Notification in the 12 Months Preceding the Survey (n = 2,038)

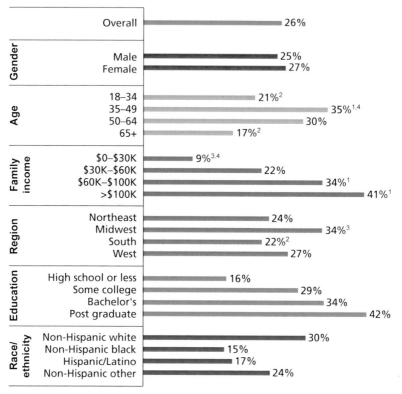

NOTE: [1,2,3] or [4] denotes statistically significant differences from the noted group, within a demographic category. Significance was calculated at $p < 0.05$ for all noted differences using the Wald test. See Figure B.2 for a different view of these data (specifically, the percentages based on population of those who reported having ever received a breach notification in their lifetime, compared with the total survey population shown here).
RAND RR1187-2.2

ogy in the past year. In addition, many of the recent "mega-breaches" (e.g., Target, Anthem Blue Cross) were suffered by companies that cater to millions of individuals.[7]

---

[7] Compare this with another mega-breach, that of the Office of Personnel Management (disclosed to the public *after* our survey had ended), in which the stolen personal data were

The increase of notices in the 12 months prior to the survey may also be a function of short-term versus long-term memory and greater awareness of data breaches. Furthermore, this value likely underestimates the true volume of breach notifications for a number of reasons. For example, some consumers may be unable to recall receiving a notice, may conflate multiple notices received for different incidents at a similar point in time, or may not have actually received (or read) a notice when they otherwise should have.

Given the prevalence of breach notices, the frequency of notifications sent to the same individual has important implications for public policy and consumer behavior. In particular, the estimated 64 million breach notifications in the 12 months from June 2014 to June 2015 raises the concern that many commentators have suggested[8]—that consumers may become desensitized to the notices and either discount them or ignore important information contained in the notices. To address this concern, we asked respondents *how many* breach notices they had received within the past 12 months.[9]

Figure 2.3 reveals that more than one-half (51 percent) of those respondents—an estimated 36 million adults—received multiple notifications, suggesting that breach notifications are, indeed, becoming a more common occurrence for many Americans.[10] This is perhaps informed by changes in some state laws that aim to make notices more actionable and informative.[11] For example, effective January 1, 2014, California requires notifying organizations to offer identity-theft protection and mitigation services to affected individuals (State Legislature

---

restricted to those who had some interaction with the federal government, either as current or former employees or as those who had undergone background checks.

[8] See, for example, recent news articles from *NPR* (Hu, 2014), *Washington Post* (Halzack, 2014), and *Wall Street Journal* (Perlberg, 2014).

[9] We acknowledge that the responses received may reflect a lower number than may be true, as participants may have stopped noticing or remembering data breaches. This is called *habituation*.

[10] The 95-percent confidence interval rests between 32.3 million and 40.5 million, based on the 2014 U.S. adult population of 245.2 million (see U.S. Census Bureau, undated).

[11] See, for example, BakerHostetler, undated, which provides updates to data breach-notification laws.

Figure 2.3
How Many Notices Have You Received in the Past 12 Months (of Those Who Had Ever Received a Notification in Their Lifetime, n = 998)?

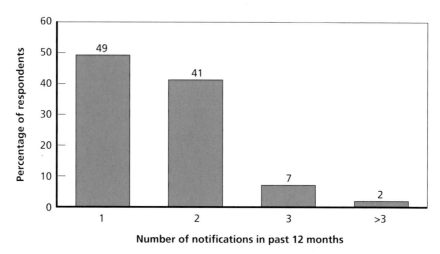

NOTE: Due to rounding, the numbers shown do not sum to 100 percent.
RAND *RR1187-2.3*

of California, 2014b) and requires victims of medical data breaches to be notified within five days (instead of 15; State Legislature of California, 2014a). Even more recently, new California laws enacted in October 2015 release companies from notifying consumers if breached data had been encrypted and include clarifying and standardizing language to breach notifications ("Changes to California's Data Breach Notification Requirements," 2015).

How Respondents Learned of a Breach

We asked whether respondents were aware of a breach before they received formal notification. As shown in Table 2.1, 56 percent of respondents who recalled having received a breach notification from a company anytime in their lifetime indicated that they first learned of a breach directly from the affected company. However, of those who became aware of a breach *before* they received notification, the most

Table 2.1
How Respondents Learned About a Data Breach (Percentage of Respondents Who Recalled Having Been Notified About a Data Breach in Their Lifetime)

	Method of Notification			
	From the Company Directly	Identified Suspicious Activity	Notified by Third Party/Bank	Heard Media Reports
Overall	56	10	16	28
Comfort level with modern technology				
Very	$55^{3,4}$	10^{4}	16	$30^{3,4}$
Moderate	$53^{3,4}$	10^{4}	18	$31^{3,4}$
Somewhat	$73^{1,2}$	9	13	16^{+}
Not at all	$77^{1,2}$	$3^{1,2}$	18	3^{+}

NOTE: Participants were able to check all that applied, so percentages may sum to more than 100 percent.

[+] denotes statistically significant differences from all other comfort-level groups (rows), within the way that participants found out (columns). [1, 2, 3,] or [4] denotes statistically significant differences from the comfort-level groups (rows), within the ways that participants found out (columns). For example, among those who first learned about the breach from the company directly, there was statistical difference between those who reported "very" or "moderate" levels of comfort with modern technology compared with those who reported "somewhat" or "not at all." For those who first learned about the data breach by identifying suspicious behavior, those who were "very" or "moderately" comfortable with modern technology had significant differences from those who had a comfort level of "not at all." Significance was calculated at $p < 0.05$ for all noted differences using the Wald test.

common method that participants recalled was through media reports (28 percent), followed by notifications from a third party, such as a bank (16 percent). Only 10 percent of respondents discovered there had been a breach by identifying suspicious activity.

There may be several reasons that individuals are learning about breaches before they receive official notifications: First, not all companies are required to disclose that a breach has occurred;[12] second, data

---

[12] For example, health care companies are required to notify individuals only if the breach affects more than 500 individuals.

breach disclosure laws vary widely by state, providing exceptions when information is lost but encrypted, for example; third, companies are not always the first to discover that a breach occurred. In fact, 70 to 80 percent of data breaches are discovered by an unrelated third party (Verizon, 2014). The media's large role in consumers' knowledge of data breaches is a trend that is expected to continue. The number of notable and high-profile breaches that have made mainstream media headlines has increased significantly over the past several years, and it is becoming more commonplace to report on breaches.[13]

There was little variation on data breach discovery by gender, age, income, or region. There were two small differences between levels of income and age. However, one would expect to see this number of significant differences by chance alone with the number of comparisons being performed.[14] The major variation on data breach discovery was by comfort level with technology, as shown in Table 2.1. The less comfortable with technology that respondents were, the more likely they were to recall hearing of the breach from the company directly.[15] The pattern was similar by educational attainment, but less pronounced. On the one hand, people who were more tech-comfortable and had higher levels of education may be more likely to be aware of how and where their data are being stored, or they may be more likely to be quicker to learn about a breach (from the media or by noticing suspicious activity, for example). On the other hand, some studies have shown that those with higher levels of education often believe that they are less vulnerable (Wash and Rader, 2015).

---

[13] See, for example, Google Trends search activity for "cyber attack" and "data breach" at www.google.com/trends/.

[14] For all details about responses by demographics, see Table B.2.

[15] The proportions hearing from the company directly are statistically different from each other for "very" and "moderately" comfortable with technology against those who are "somewhat" or "not at all" comfortable at the 10-percent level (but the differences within very/moderately and somewhat/not at all are not statistically different).

Types of Data Compromised

There have been many breaches involving large-scale loss or theft of many different forms of data, including credit cards (e.g., Target), Social Security numbers (e.g., Anthem), medical information (e.g., TRICARE), mortgage information (e.g., Countrywide), user account data (e.g., Sony PlayStation), and sensitive personnel data (e.g., the Office of Personnel Management). However, there is a relatively small body of research on the different forms of data compromised in these breaches (Romanosky, Hoffman, and Acquisti, 2014). Therefore, we asked respondents to identify the types of data lost in the most-recent breach notification they received. The responses for 998 individuals are shown in Table 2.2.[16]

Table 2.2
What Types of Information Were Lost or Stolen (n = 998)?

Type of Information	Respondents (%)
Credit card information	49
Non–credit card financial information	10
Health information	21
Social Security number	17
User account information	13
Other personal information	13
Not sure—company never told me	18
Not sure—I don't remember	9

NOTE: Percentages do not sum to 100 because respondents were permitted to select multiple types of information.

---

[16] Of the 2,038 individuals who answered the survey, 998 answered "yes" to question 1 (have you ever received a notification). These were the individuals of whom we asked questions related to types of information lost/stolen; therefore, data are representative of the 998 individuals only.

As shown, credit card information is the most common type of information compromised.[17] This, along with other financial data (such as bank account numbers), can be changed, although at some cost to both firms and consumers. What is far more concerning is that a significant percentage (at least 21 percent) of the participants reported having information taken that is difficult, if not impossible, to change, such as health information, Social Security numbers, and other personal information.[18] Health information, such as date and place of birth, blood type, and health history, cannot be changed, and changing a Social Security number, or personal information, such as a physical home address and mother's maiden name, can be slow, complex, and comes at a great cost. From an attacker's perspective, these latter types of data can be used to conduct identity theft or medical fraud or can be used for better targeting, more-specific spearphishing campaigns, and possible blackmail or espionage activities.

It is also surprising that 18 percent of respondents indicated that they were never informed of the types of information compromised. Without this basic information, it can be difficult for consumers to take action. While it may be straightforward to guard against potential identity theft or future abuse of one's information, it clearly becomes more difficult and costly without sufficient information concerning the kind of data lost or stolen.

---

[17] That credit card information was the most-reported type of information stolen is a departure from other studies of compromised data. A NetDiligence study using anonymous cyber insurance claim data from 2014 reported that personal information was the most frequently exposed type of data (41 percent of breaches, n = 117), followed by personal health information (21 percent) and then credit card information (19 percent) (NetDiligence, 2014). Further, Romanosky, Hoffman, and Acquisti, 2014, found that the most-common personal information stolen was name, address, and Social Security number (77 percent of breaches, n = 1,772), followed by credit card and health information (12 percent).

[18] We cannot comment on the absolute percentage of respondents who lost such information because of the potential overlap between discrete categories of information.

Consumer Responses to the Breach

Many companies that have experienced a breach employ the services of a data breach resolution provider, such as AllClear (used by Anthem) or CSID (used by the Office of Personnel Management), that will monitor consumer accounts for credit or identity fraud. The data breach resolution provider hired by the affected company is not only responsible for performing credit monitoring but also responsible for sending out notifications to consumers and providing call center support.[19] Some providers offer a bulk rate discount, charging 25 cents per person per year (Conn, 2015), while other providers will charge based only on the number of individuals who sign up, which previous studies have shown to be low. An official at Experian, a leader in consumer identity-theft protection services, noted that the number is often less than 10 percent ("Amid Rampant Data Theft, Consumers Left Breached and Burned Out," 2015). A 2014 report (Ponemon Institute, 2014) noted that only 29 percent of consumers accepted protection measures offered. A 2015 report by the Bureau of Justice Statistics (Harrell, 2015) found that less than 10 percent of victims purchase identity-theft protection (4 percent) or purchased identity-theft insurance or used a credit monitoring service (6 percent).[20] One possible explanation for the low percentages, especially compared with our survey results, could be due to consumers incorrectly recalling that they had accepted offers, overestimating the number they had accepted, or perhaps conflating multiple offers in which they only accepted one. On the other hand, such companies as Experian may not always be aware of how banks distribute information

---

[19] Based on author's phone communications with head of security and privacy at a large public relations firm (July 2015).

[20] It is important to note that, while these all relate to the use of identity or credit monitoring services, there are some differences between these studies. For example, there is no information about methodology for Experian's response (the official was quoted in a news article); both the Ponemon report and Experian response are from the point of view of the company, while our survey and the findings of the Bureau of Justice Statistics are from the point of view of the consumer; and the Bureau of Justice Statistics asked about the victim purchasing protection, rather than it being offered for free (as in the other cases).

or services and thus may underestimate how many offers consumers are accepting.

To validate these estimates of consumer participation in prevention services, we asked respondents about the different remediation approaches offered by breached companies and what attitudes they had concerning those approaches, focusing on the most-recent breach notification.

Consumer Redress

We asked respondents whether the breached company offered free credit monitoring or another type of assistance to mitigate potential losses. Table 2.3 shows that, overall, people were offered assistance 60 percent of the time; however, those who lost health information recalled receiving such offers 80 percent of the time. This increase may be a result of stolen health care data being recognized as nonfungible and thus posing a greater threat to the victim than other data losses (e.g., a credit card, which can be more easily replaced). While it is true that identity-theft monitoring would not prevent abuse of health information itself, medical identity theft is still a significant concern.

Next, we asked individuals who had ever received a breach notification about their most-recent notification and acceptance of credit monitoring offers. For those who had been offered free credit monitoring or other assistance, as Figure 2.4 shows—and contrary to the extremely low acceptance rate previously described—a staggering 62 percent of

Table 2.3
Were You Offered Credit Monitoring or Other Types of Assistance (n = 998)?

	Yes	No	Not Sure
Overall	60%	30%	10%
If credit card information was taken	61%	31%	8%
If health information was taken	80%	12%	8%
If information other than credit card or health information was taken	58%	30%	12%

Figure 2.4
Did You Accept the Offer for Assistance (Percentage of Those Who Had Been Offered Identity Theft or Credit Monitoring Services, in Relation to Their Most-Recent Notification, n = 998)?

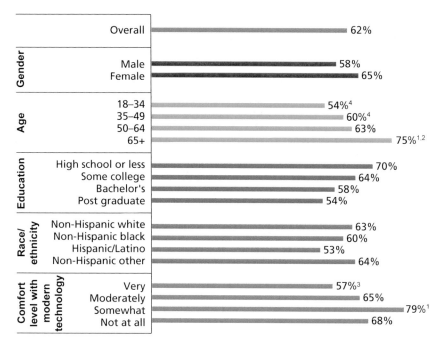

NOTE: [1, 2, 3,] or [4] denotes statistically significant differences from the noted group, within a demographic category. Significance was calculated at $p < 0.05$ for all noted differences using the Wald test.

RAND *RR1187-2.4*

individuals accepted the offers.[21] Those who are female, older, less educated, or non-Hispanic were more likely to accept the offers.

When respondents were asked why they accepted the offer (or not), three common themes emerged: (1) time and effort required, (2) quality perception and trust (both of the affected company and of the breach-notification service), and (3) overlapping identity-theft ser-

---

[21] Another possibility for the difference in percentages compared with other studies could be due to methodology: In our survey, we asked participants who had already received offers who accepted, whereas other studies may have taken the percentage out of the entire population of those affected (who may not have been offered).

vice offers. For people who *did* accept, common reasons included the following:

- no risk or cost perceived: "It's free, why not?" One person even wrote, "Asking why I accepted it seems a little odd."
- to prevent future fraud, to take caution, and for better peace of mind (for example, "To sleep better at night," and "Due Diligence").
- to hold the company accountable: "Companies need to be held accountable for their security failures."
- no choice: "I was informed that I was automatically signed up for this service."

For people who *did not* accept, a greater variety of reasons were given:

- duplication of a similar monitoring service: "I already have a credit alert"; "I was still receiving credit monitoring from another company that had suffered a data breach previously."
- duplication of personal effort: "I personally monitor my accounts closely."
- uncertainty of quality of service and wariness of offer: "They also wanted my credit card info. I thought it was a scam."
- lack of trust in the company: "I did not trust the company anymore."
- did not seem necessary: "I checked my account and nothing was missing"; "I wasn't interested."
- seemed like a hassle or too much work: "Laziness"; "Basic Apathy"; "Hassle."
- no time, or forgetfulness: "I did not have time to follow up"; "I haven't gotten around to it yet but intend to"; "I procrastinated until after the offer expired"; "I simply forgot to register."
- unable to accept: "I tried to accept the offer but couldn't successfully sign up on their website."

Those in the baby boomer generation (age 65+) may have accepted at such a high rate (especially compared with Gen Xers or millennials—those considered "digital natives") because this group (which includes retirees) may have more time to follow up with such offers, or perhaps because they take data breaches more seriously than other age groups. In addition, given that only 27 percent of the 65+ age demographic felt "very comfortable" with modern technology, they may be more reassured by having a third party help detect identity fraud. Finally, it may be the case that digital natives have become more desensitized to their personal data being available to others (intentionally, such as through social media; or unintentionally, such as through data breaches).

Interestingly, the percentage of respondents accepting offers declined with education level. Conceivably, one may think that more-educated users would be more aware of potential risks and therefore more likely to avail themselves of free offers.

Another notable difference among respondents is that, generally, those who are less comfortable with modern technology are more likely to accept assistance. Conceivably, the more sophisticated one is with technology, the more able one is to manage one's affairs without assistance. Alternatively, this same group may also conduct more activity online, receive more notifications, and therefore have already accepted offers of assistance.

It may be the case that those who declined (or ignored) offers perceived the offers as simply a risk of making their information available to yet another company (because many data protection companies ask for sensitive personal and account information in order to monitor).

It is unclear whether duplication of credit monitoring or identity-theft prevention services would impose substantial inefficiencies or unnecessary social costs, so the particular policy recommendation requires additional analysis. However, if these services are effective at preventing or reducing consumer losses, these responses suggest that both consumers and firms can take additional actions to ensure greater acceptance and reduce overall losses. For example, to the extent that individuals are discouraged from accepting these offers because of the perceived (or actual) effort or because of perceived ineffectiveness, the process of enrollment could be made easier, and clear benefits could be better communicated.

Consumer Attrition

A critical corporate and policy issue concerns consumer attrition in the event of a data breach: Are consumers closing financial accounts or choosing to shop elsewhere after learning of a data breach, or are they willing to remain loyal to the breached company? Clearly, there are many reasons that an individual would cease ties with a firm after receiving a breach notification. However, in practice, this may not always be wise, or practical. For example, while it may be simple to shop at a competing retailer, the switching costs incurred from changing health insurers, mortgage companies, or employers may be prohibitive. Further, there may be no practical alternative (e.g., in the case of Facebook or Google) or choice (e.g., the Office of Personnel Management). In addition, even if an individual did wish to change businesses (a bank, for example), he or she would be required to provide the same personal information to yet another company, and there may be a lack of comparative data to assess whether competitors are doing a better job. In effect, one could argue that such a person would only be *increasing* his or her chances of future compromise of personal data.

To better understand consumer response following a breach, we asked individuals whether they stopped dealing with the company following the breach about which they were most recently notified. As illustrated in Figure 2.5, our results show that 11 percent of respondents stopped interacting with the affected organization after being notified of a breach, leaving 89 percent of respondents who chose to remain.[22] While the majority (65 percent) said that the data breach did not affect the amount of business they give the organization, 23 percent said that they gave them less business than before. Interestingly, 1 percent said that they actually gave the organization more business following the breach.[23]

---

[22] Including those who gave less, more, and the same amount of business.

[23] We acknowledge that 1 percent (approximately nine respondents) may be in scope of people not really paying attention to the survey and clicking through questions to finish.

Figure 2.5
Consumer Patronage of Company After the Most Recently
Notified Breach (of Those Who Had Ever Received a Breach
Notification, n = 998)

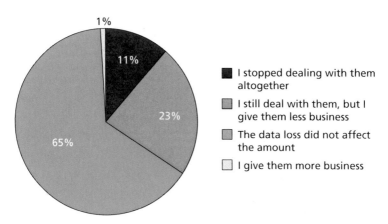

1%

11%

23%

65%

■ I stopped dealing with them
   altogether

▨ I still deal with them, but I
   give them less business

▨ The data loss did not affect
   the amount

☐ I give them more business

NOTE: Due to rounding, the numbers shown do not sum to 100 percent.
RAND *RR1187-2.5*

The fact that consumers continue to conduct business with these companies is revealing, especially because organizations are not always able to remediate their breaches immediately—if ever. Consider, for example, a Ponemon study that found that 20 percent of information technology security practitioners reported that they were unable to determine whether a breach was ever resolved (Ponemon Institute, 2015).

That the overwhelming majority of consumers (89 percent) continue to do business with the breached company appears to provide little incentive for the company to change its behavior, especially with regard to cybersecurity protection or defenses. While chief information security officers—i.e., those who are typically in charge of protecting company and personal information—place a high value on the reputation of their company (Libicki, Ablon, and Webb, 2015), these responses suggest that customers either are not put off by breaches or are becoming desensitized to them. In other words, the "sunlight" brought to the company through required notifications may not be having much effect on consumers. Indeed, information disclosure can be a useful policy device, but only to the extent that those consuming the information care about it.

Consumers reporting that the company or organization either lost their business altogether or received less of their business than before as a result of the data breach varied across subgroups. Non-Hispanic blacks were the most likely to claim that the data breach led to a loss or decrease in business (53 percent), a much greater rate than that for non-Hispanic whites.

Respondents whose health information was compromised were less likely to stop conducting business with the affected company than those whose credit card information was taken (27 percent versus 37 percent, respectively). Given that it is much easier to change credit card numbers than primary health care facilities or established trust relationships with individual doctors, this is unsurprising.

See Figure B.1 for more analysis by gender, age, ethnicity, income, and type of data compromised.

Consumer Actions to Improve Data Protection After a Breach

As mentioned, one of the primary motivations behind information disclosure in general, and data breach notification specifically, is to empower consumers to take action to prevent further—or future—harm. However, humans suffer from many psychological biases that can prevent or hinder any action at all (Hoch and Loewenstein, 1991; Loewenstein, John, and Volpp, 2012; Romanosky, Telang, and Acquisti, 2011). Indeed, providing actionable and timely information in a manner that overcomes these challenges has been a difficult policy issue in many sectors. For example, these same biases affect consumer understanding and decisionmaking with regard to disclosure notices for financial products, and many attempts have been made to improve consumer understanding of such notices (Beshears et al., 2011; Garrison et al., 2012; Consumer Financial Protection Bureau, 2013). Further, the number of consumers who file police reports or take legal action when they become fraud victims is decreasing, although many consumers claim to install antispyware or firewalls on their computers (Javelin Strategy and Research, 2011).

In order to inform the policy debate about consumer actions and perceptions in response to data breaches, our survey posed questions about the steps that respondents recalled taking to prevent any potential effects from the most recently notified data breach. As Table 2.4 shows, 51 percent of respondents changed their password or personal identification number (PIN), while 22 percent of respondents took no action at all.

Respondents were also provided an opportunity to provide more information. Some common responses included the following:

- paid with cash more often
- greater awareness all around: "Added alerts to other existing accounts," "monitored credit card activity more closely for several months afterwards," "increased monitoring of all accounts from once a week to 3x a week," and "required personal (phone) approval on all new accounts"
- asked for new cards to be issued, regardless of whether those accounts were related to the breach
- ran antivirus scans on computers and systems.

Those who took *no* action provided additional explanations:

- "Unable to take action because medical information was hacked."
- "I cannot change my health insurance."
- "Because it was my employer's site that was hacked, there was nothing any of us could do but wait and see what happens."

Some respondents simply did not care enough about the particular account. For example, one individual who suffered a breach to his/her university account noted that "nothing was financially important." This type of response suggests that some respondents give less attention to data that are not financial. However, studies have shown that nonfinancial information, such as account credentials (username and password combination), can be considered more valuable and often command a higher price on the cybercrime black market (Ablon, Libicki,

Table 2.4
What Actions Did You Take to Prevent Potential Effects of the Breach (based on the Most Recent Breach Notification, for Respondents Who Had Ever Received a Breach Notification, n = 998)?

	Changed Password or PIN	Notified Others	Started Using a Password Manager	Stopped Shopping at Website or Store	Closed or Switched Account	Became More Diligent	Took No Action
Overall	51%	17%	4%	13%	24%	24%	22%
Gender							
Male	53%	15%	3%	16%	25%	23%	25%
Female	50%	20%	4%	11%	24%	26%	20%
Age							
18–34	49%	22%	4%	13%	18%[2,4]	18%[3,4]	25%
35–49	50%	16%	3%	11%	28%[1]	19%[3,4]	27%[3]
50–64	56%	15%	4%	14%	24%	28%[1,2]	18%[2]
65+	46%	17%	4%	17%	31%[1]	37%[1,2]	18%
Family Income							
$0–$30K	48%	20%	2%[2]	14%	18%	21%	25%
$30K–$60K	52%	18%	5%[1]	16%	21%	26%	19%
$60K–$100K	55%	20%	2%	15%	26%	22%	24%
>$100K	49%	14%	5%	10%	27%	26%	22%

Table 2.4—Continued

	Changed Password or PIN	Notified Others	Started Using a Password Manager	Stopped Shopping at Website or Store	Closed or Switched Account	Became More Diligent	Took No Action
Education							
High school or less	52%	17%	2%[4]	11%	17%[2]	22%	25%
Some college	50%	18%	4%	17%	30%[1]	25%	21%
Bachelor's	51%	17%	4%	11%	25%	26%	19%
Postgraduate	52%	16%	6%[1]	15%	24%	24%	24%

NOTE: [1], [2], [3], or [4] denotes statistically significant differences from the noted group, within a demographic category. Calculations were done for each column (actions taken) independently. Note that there are few significant relationships other than those in the age demographic category: In particular, those aged 50+ reported being more likely to be more diligent (about accounts, clicking links and attachments) than those aged 18–49. This may be because members of the younger age group already were diligent, so did not become more diligent. Significance was calculated at p < 0.05 for all noted differences using the Wald test.

and Golay, 2014)—although it can be difficult for users to understand or perceive this risk.

Consumer Costs of Dealing with a Data Breach

There are many potential costs that an individual may bear following a data breach, such as nonreimbursed theft of money from checking or savings accounts, time and money spent repairing any damaged credit accounts, lost wages, or the transaction cost incurred from finding a new company with the same services. While establishing accurate estimates of these losses has been notoriously hard, we asked respondents to offer their subjective assessments of the dollar value–equivalent cost to them as a result of a data breach. When asked "If you could place a dollar value on the amount of displeasure and inconvenience that you experienced as a result of this data loss/theft, what would it be?" 32 percent of respondents reported that the breach imposed no dollar loss to them, and, for those who reported a loss, the median was $500 (see Table 2.5).

We found consistency across other subgroups with the exception of education and family income: While the percentage responding zero was very similar across educational groups, the median dollar value decreased with higher levels of education and a higher family income. Median dollar values were also higher in cases in which health information, Social Security number, or other financial information was compromised.

Not shown in the table are the extreme responses. Just under 6 percent of respondents reported that the inconvenience cost them $10,000 or more. This is a nontrivial group of people, because this represents about 6 million U.S. adults.[24] Interestingly, those in the 18–34 age category were significantly less likely to be extreme responders than older age groups. Those with graduate degrees were significantly less likely to be extreme responders than those with less than a high school diploma. Based on the percentage differences of those who reported

---

[24] The 95-percent confidence interval rests between 4.3 million and 7.6 million, based on the 2014 U.S. adult population of 245.2 million (U.S. Census Bureau, undated).

Table 2.5
What Is Your Estimated Dollar Value–Equivalent Cost of Dealing with the Breach?

Category	Percentage Responding $0	25th Percentile (if >$0)	Median (if >$0)	75th Percentile (if >$0)	Maximum
Overall	32%	$100	$500	$1,000	$9.00×10^{18}
Gender					
Male	32%	$100	$500	$1,000	$1.00×10^{15}
Female	31%	$100	$250	$1,000	$9.00×10^{18}
Age					
18–34	32%	$50	$100	$500	$100,000
35–49	29%	$100	$500	$1,200	$9.00×10^{18}
50–64	32%	$100	$500	$2,000	$1.00×10^{13}
65+	33%	$100	$500	$2,000	$1.00×10^{16}
Family Income					
$0–$30K	31%	$100	$500	$2,000	$9.00×10^{18}
$30K–$60K	38%	$100	$500	$5,000	$1.00×10^{16}
$60K–$100K	24%	$100	$200	$1,000	$1.00×10^{13}
>$100K	34%	$100	$250	$1,000	$1.00×10^{9}

Table 2.5—Continued

Category	Percentage Responding $0	25th Percentile (if >$0)	Median (if >$0)	75th Percentile (if >$0)	Maximum
Region					
Northeast	27%	$100	$250	$1,000	1.00×10^{10}
Midwest	33%	$50	$200	$1,000	1.00×10^{8}
South	34%	$100	$500	$1,000	$1,000,000
West	30%	$100	$500	$1,500	9.00×10^{18}
Education					
High school or less	30%	$100	$500	$5,000	1.00×10^{11}
Some college	34%	$100	$500	$1,000	9.00×10^{18}
Bachelor's	30%	$100	$250	$1,000	1.00×10^{16}
Postgraduate	31%	$50	$200	$1,000	1.00×10^{9}
Race/ethnicity					
Non-Hispanic white	34%	$100	$250	$1,000	1.00×10^{16}
Non-Hispanic black	22%	$100	$1,000	$2,000	9.00×10^{18}
Hispanic/Latino	29%	$100	$500	$5,000	1.00×10^{13}
Non-Hispanic other	21%	$100	$864	$2,000	2.00×10^{8}

Table 2.5—Continued

Category	Percentage Responding $0	25th Percentile (if >$0)	Median (if >$0)	75th Percentile (if >$0)	Maximum
Type of information compromised					
Credit card information	30%	$100	$500	$1,000	$9.00×10^{18}
Other financial information	31%	$300	$864	$2,000	$100,000
Health information	29%	$100	$1,000	$5,000	$9.00×10^{18}
Social Security number	27%	$200	$1,000	$10,000	$9.00×10^{18}
User account information	25%	$50	$500	$2,500	$1,000,000
Other personal information	25%	$100	$500	$5,000	$1.00×10^{11}
Unsure—company didn't tell me	32%	$50	$500	$1,000	$1.00×10^{13}
Unsure—don't remember	40%	$35	$100	$1,000	$500,000

experiencing an extreme inconvenience, equal percentages identified the loss of credit card data and the loss of health information as the most important cause, followed by compromised Social Security numbers and other personal information.[25]

Consumer Satisfaction with Company Response to the Breach

Companies can engage in a variety of post-breach activities in an attempt to assuage customers, employees, potential plaintiffs, federal and state regulators, and, in certain cases, Congress. However, it is unclear which approaches are most effective in which circumstances, and which actions will have the greatest effects over the short and long terms on firm profits, customer retention, and regulatory oversight. To better understand customer preferences, we asked survey respondents to rate their levels of satisfaction with the firm's response to the breach and to rate their satisfaction with a list of breach responses companies might consider.

Figure 2.6 shows the overall satisfaction rate of those surveyed. We found that the vast majority (77 percent) expressed satisfaction with the firm's breach response. There was some variation by subgroup, as shown in the figure. The greatest differences were by race/ethnicity: Minorities were much less likely to claim that they were satisfied, were more likely to place a higher dollar value on the inconvenience caused by the breach, and were more likely to cease doing business with the company.

Next, we asked respondents to rate their preference for six alternative breach response actions along a six-point Likert scale, as shown Table 2.6. Individuals valued three measures more highly than financial compensation for the inconvenience: (1) ensuring that a breach does not occur in the future, (2) offering free credit monitoring or

---

[25] This was a bit surprising, because we expected to find that those who lost nonreplaceable data (e.g., date of birth, Social Security number) put the most value on the inconvenience (rather than those whose credit card information was stolen and just needed to get a new number). There are no significant differences between the demographic or comfort level with technology groups. This may be largely because the sample size for each of these is small, and there is limited variation in medians.

Figure 2.6
Were You Satisfied with the Firm's Breach Response to the Most Recent Breach Notification (Consumers Who Had Ever Received a Breach Notification, n = 998)?

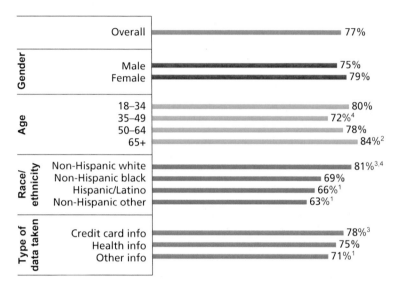

NOTE: [1, 2, 3,] or [4] denotes statistically significant differences from the noted group, within a demographic category. Significance was calculated at $p < 0.05$ for all noted differences using the Wald test.
RAND *RR1187-2.6*

similar services to ensure that lost data are not misused, and (3) notifying consumers immediately. The least-satisfactory responses a company could take were donating money to organizations that promote cybersecurity and simply apologizing to those affected.

When offered the opportunity to elaborate on their responses, respondents commonly described the following:

- provide advice on what I can do to better protect my data
- more openness and details from the company of what happened and how: "Tell the truth without spin"; "be very specific about communications"; "provide more detail"; "Just be honest and

inform me exactly what happened, why it happened, and how they plan on safe guarding data so it doesn't happen again"
• reimburse for all fraudulent charges
• keep me informed on what new measures the company is implementing to prevent future breaches.

Table 2.6
How Satisfied Would You Be with the Following Breach Responses?

Action	Not Improve Satisfaction				Greatly Improve Satisfaction	
	0	1	2	3	4	5
Apologize	21%	10%	11%	19%	15%	24%
Notify immediately	4%	2%	5%	10%	17%	63%
Take measures to prevent future breach	4%	1%	4%	8%	15%	68%
Donate money to organizations that promote cybersecurity	29%	16%	16%	18%	10%	11%
Compensate for any financial loss	6%	4%	8%	13%	15%	54%
Offer credit monitoring or other assistance	4%	2%	4%	9%	17%	64%

CHAPTER THREE

Conclusions and Implications

Based on the results from this novel survey, an estimated 105 million U.S. adults (43 percent of the U.S. adult population[1]) reported receiving a breach notification in their lifetime. Further, within the 12 months prior to this survey (June 2014–June 2015), an estimated 64 million U.S. adults received a breach notification, and 36 million received two or more. That being a victim of a data breach—and often multiple data breaches—is so common speaks to the increasing reliance that all sectors (retail, health care, finance, etc.) have on digital technology, as well as the ease with which tools for hacking can be purchased and used (Ablon, Libicki, and Golay, 2014; Cárdenas et al., 2009).

A surprising 44 percent of respondents learned of the breach from other sources before they received an official breach notification. This suggests that media reports, banks, and credit monitoring services, among others, play an important role in informing consumers of data breaches and that firms could improve their response in order to best manage publicity concerning the breach. However, this finding raises a crucial tension regarding the optimal time for disclosure of risk (in this case, risk of consumer identity theft). On one hand, prompt notification of potential harm can help reduce consumer losses. On the other hand, notifying individuals too soon may be impractical for the company (i.e., there may simply not be enough information available concerning the cause or scope of the breach), and it may jeopardize

---

[1] Based on the 2014 U.S. adult population of 245.2 million (see U.S. Census Bureau, undated).

ongoing law enforcement investigations. Thus, the optimal time for consumer notification of a data breach remains unclear.[2]

Sixty-two percent of respondents accepted the offer of free credit monitoring or similar services. This high acceptance rate is startling, given previous claims that only a small percentage of consumers avail themselves of such offers—although recall ability of consumers versus reported information from companies and multiple-notification conflation could be explanations for the differences. The high rate of acceptance provides one rebuttal to claims that consumers are apathetic or unconcerned about data breaches and potential risks from the compromise of their personal information. Furthermore, of participants who reported not having accepted offers, many cited their reason as already having such a service. Indeed, this is exactly the sort of action that was intended with the breach-notification laws and therefore should be welcomed by policymakers. These consumer actions should also be comforting to breached firms that are providing such assistance. Given that past research has shown that firms are less likely to be sued when they provide credit monitoring (Romanosky, Hoffman, and Acquisti, 2014), higher acceptance rates will likely further help reduce civil litigation costs.

Although our data on financial losses are somewhat limited, responses suggest that a substantial number of consumers experience (what they perceive to be) little to no financial loss, while a smaller number of consumers experience what they perceive as large losses. This distribution (i.e., many individuals perceiving no loss, with a few estimating high loss) is not unexpected and generally mirrors actual (median) financial losses as recorded by other studies (Harrell and Langton, 2013). One advantage of soliciting consumer responses of perceived loss from a privacy event, such as a data breach, is that it may more fully incorporate the variety of negative sentiments and reactions associated with data breaches[3] than soliciting strictly financial loss information. If this survey's findings had indicated perceived losses

---

[2]   There is a similar ongoing debate regarding the appropriate time for public disclosure of software vulnerabilities that has yet to be settled.

[3]   For example, feelings of loss of privacy or fears of future harm.

of thousands of dollars (as opposed to hundreds of dollars), this might indicate more pressing and unresolved issues. That said, the impact of data losses may not be obvious to consumers, nor immediately available or traceable. Thus, there are reasons to question whether the assessments of no or little loss have merit, while those reporting actual numbers are more likely to be sharing information about the losses of which they have actual knowledge.

When examining customer reactions and sentiments following a breach, we found that consumer attrition is only 11 percent, and consumers seem to appreciate companies that respond and appear to take responsibility for breaches they suffer. The overwhelming majority of respondents highly value prompt notification of data breaches, and an even larger majority of respondents continued to do business with the breached company. However, it is unclear whether this customer loyalty is truly the result of customer appreciation or whether the actual (or perceived) costs of switching firms (e.g., health care provider, employer) are sufficiently high, pinning the individual to the firm. Together, these results suggest two things: First, beyond emphasizing preventive measures, regulations might focus on how a breached company can more immediately notify the consumer and keep him or her informed of remediation efforts; second, firms may have little incentive to change (or improve) their breach response practices, either because consumers are entirely content or because consumers are unable or unwilling to shift their business. One important implication of low customer attrition and high satisfaction with company notification and breach response is that companies appear to be taking their responsibilities seriously.

Furthermore, shaming of breached companies by media outlets may be useful only for those companies that have not provided notification and may be more harmful than good for those who have (as they may be working to build back their reputation and patch their security posture, so negative media would be only a detriment), especially because customer attrition is low and satisfaction with notification and breach response is high. Rather, media outlets can help by providing consumers with useful information about what next steps they should take.

Can a Federal Breach Disclosure Law Help?

Although many states have passed legislation requiring companies to notify consumers after a breach is detected, requirements vary across jurisdictions, and three states do not yet have such mandates. In reaction to the burden of investigating and complying with 47 disparate state laws, many firms have lobbied for a single—i.e., federal—breach-notification law. In January 2015, the White House proposed the Personal Data Notification and Protection Act, which would supersede current state data breach-notification laws, creating a single national standard "checklist" to follow (Office of the Press Secretary, 2015). The Senate introduced its own bill at the same time, the Data Security and Breach Notification Act of 2015 (114th Congress, 2015a), which would require companies to notify federal agencies and individuals of any breach that affects more than 5,000 customers (Levin, 2015). In May 2015, Representatives Randy Neugebauer and John Carney introduced a bill, the Data Security Act of 2015, that would help standardize breach notifications from financial institutions and retailers. At the same time, member of the Senate introduced a companion bill (114th Congress, 2015b).

The benefits of a federal law range and may depend on the stakeholder: consumer, companies, and federal and state law enforcement and regulators. First, it is unclear whether or how a federal law benefits consumers over current state laws. For others, national law could simplify the policies that a company must follow, may facilitate law enforcement investigation, and could help smaller businesses that operate across state lines and that do not have the resources to navigate the myriad of state-specific laws. However, as some argue, a federal data breach law might reduce the effectiveness of regulators at the state level and should not preempt state enforcement (Newcombe, 2014). For example, it is uncertain whether federal standards would be a floor or a ceiling; some states may want stricter standards. If a federal statute were only to impose a minimum notification floor and not preempt any of the state laws, there would still be variation across all the states. In effect, a federal law could well result in yet another disclosure law with which a compromised firm must comply.

Based on the results of our survey, consumers are most satisfied when breach notices are more timely, when they are kept up to date on remediation and improved security measures, and offered identity protection and credit monitoring services following a breach. Our survey is one data point on consumer reactions and attitudes toward breach notifications and breached companies. Other information that would be useful for researchers and policymakers to better understand the problem and find a solution include better specificity on how consumers process and understand notifications sent to them (via email, mail, phone, etc.), how consumers communicate displeasure, and how long consumers are actually upset about a breach before returning to similar behaviors from before the breach. More granularity on demographic differences would also be useful.

Survey Instrument

[This appendix contains the text of our survey instrument, which is unedited but formatted for consistency.]

The following questions explore your views regarding data breaches and loss or theft of personal information.

1. Have you ever been notified by a company that your personal information may have been lost by them or stolen from them due to a hack or data breach? (Yes/No)

(If yes to 1) 2. Were you aware that your personal information was lost/stolen before being notified by the company? (check all that apply)
   (Opt1) Yes—I found out myself (e.g., suspicious behavior on credit card, locked out of accounts, etc.)
   (Opt2) Yes—I was notified by a 3rd party company (e.g., my bank or credit card company told me)
   (Opt3) Yes—I heard media reports about the data loss
   (Opt4) No—I first learned of this from the affected company

(If yes to 1) 3. Have you been notified within the past 12 months by a company that your personal information may have been lost by them or stolen from them due to a hack or data breach? (Yes/No)

(If yes to 3) 4. How many notices have you received in the past 12 months?

(If yes to 1) 5. Thinking about only the most recent time that you were notified of a potential loss/theft of personal information:

5a. What type of information was lost/stolen (check all that apply)
(Opt1) Credit card information
(Opt2) Financial information other than credit card information (e.g., bank account numbers, mortgage information)
(Opt3) Health information
(Opt4) Social Security number
(Opt5) User account information (e.g., username, password, email address)
(Opt6) Other personal data (e.g., address, mother's maiden name, etc.)
(Opt7) Not sure—the company never told me what kind of data was lost
(Opt8) Not sure—I don't remember

5b. Were you offered free credit monitoring or other assistance in dealing with the potential effects of the data loss/theft by the company that suffered the data loss? (Yes/No/Not Sure)

(If yes to 5b) 5c. Did you accept the offer? (Yes/No)

(If yes to 5b) 5d. Please explain why you did or did not accept the offer.

5e. Were you satisfied with how the loss/theft of your information was handled? (Yes/No)

5f. If you could place a dollar value on the amount of displeasure and inconvenience that you experienced as a result of this data loss/theft, what would it be?

5g. Did you personally take any of the following steps to deal with potential effects of the data loss/theft? (check all that apply)
(Opt1) Changed my passwords or PIN
(Opt2) Notified others who may also have been be affected
(Opt3) Started using a password manager
(Opt4) Stopped shopping at a particular website or retailer
(Opt5) Closed an account or switched to a new account
(Opt6) Became more wary of links and attachments in emails, etc.
(Opt7) I did not take any steps
(Opt8) Other: Please specify _____

5h. How did the hack or data breach affect your willingness to do business with the company or organization that lost your data?
(Opt1) I stopped dealing with them altogether
(Opt2) I still deal with them, but I give them less business
(Opt3) The data loss did not affect the amount of business I give them
(Opt4) I give them more business

6a. Companies take a variety of actions to resolve incidents where personal information is lost or stolen. On a scale of 0–5, where 0 represents an action that would not improve your satisfaction at all, and 5 represents an actions that would greatly improve your satisfaction, please rate the following actions in terms of how much they would affect your satisfaction with a company's response following a loss/theft of your information.
Apologize to you (0–5)
Notify you immediately (0–5)
Take measures to ensure that a similar breach cannot occur in the future (0–5)
Donate money to nonprofit organizations that promote cybersecurity (0–5)
Provide financial compensation to you for your inconvenience (0–5)
Offer credit monitoring or other measures to ensure that lost data cannot be misused (0–5)

6b. Are there any other measures that you would recommend that a company use to respond to a loss/theft of your information?

7. How comfortable do you feel using modern technology like computers, email, and cell phones?
    (Opt1) Very
    (Opt2) Moderately
    (Opt3) Somewhat
    (Opt4) Not at all

Supporting Tables and Charts

Table B.1
How Comfortable Do You Feel Using Modern Technology, Such as Computers, Email, and Cell Phones?

Category	Very	Moderately	Somewhat	Not at All	Total
Overall	49%	35%	14%	2%	100%
Gender					
Male	51%	35%	12%	3%	100%
Female	48%	35%	15%	2%	100%
Age					
18–34	67%	25%	7%	1%	100%
35–49	55%	32%	11%	2%	100%
50–64	40%	38%	18%	3%	100%
65+	27%	49%	20%	4%	100%
Family Income					
$0–$30K	40%	36%	19%	5%	100%
$30K–$60K	45%	35%	17%	3%	100%
$60K–$100K	51%	38%	11%	1%	100%
>$100K	63%	29%	7%	1%	100%
Education					
High school or less	35%	41%	20%	3%	100%
Some college	55%	31%	12%	2%	100%

Table B.1—Continued

Category	Very	Moderately	Somewhat	Not at All	Total
Bachelor's	62%	31%	6%	1%	100%
Postgraduate	65%	27%	7%	0%	100%
Region					
Northeast	47%	36%	14%	3%	100%
Midwest	47%	37%	14%	2%	100%
South	47%	36%	13%	3%	100%
West	54%	31%	14%	1%	100%
Race/ethnicity					
Non-Hispanic white	51%	34%	14%	2%	100%
Non-Hispanic black	38%	45%	15%	3%	100%
Hispanic/Latino	48%	33%	14%	5%	100%
Non-Hispanic other	61%	25%	11%	3%	100%

NOTE: Percentage totals might not sum to 100 due to rounding.

Table B.2
How Respondents Found Out About Their Last Breach

| | Method of Notification | | | |
Category	From the Company Directly	Identified Suspicious Activity	Notified by Third Party/Bank	Heard Media Reports
Overall	56%	10%	16%	28%
Gender				
Male	55%	11%	17%	26%
Female	58%	8%	15%	30%
Age				
18–34	53%	14%[3]	19%	28%
35–49	58%	8%	17%	31%
50–64	60%	7%[1]	15%	26%
65+	54%	11%	13%	30%
Family Income				
$0–$30K	52%	12%	14%	26%
$30K–$60K	55%	9%	22%	24%
$60K–$100K	63%[4]	7%	13%	28%
>$100K	53%[3]	12%	16%	32%
Region				
Northeast	55%	12%	14%	27%
Midwest	58%	6%	15%	31%
South	55%	12%	17%	28%
West	57%	9%	17%	28%
Education				
High school or less	63%	7%	15%	19%[3,4]
Some college	57%	11%	18%	25%[3,4]
Bachelor's	52%	9%	16%	37%[1,2]

Table B.2—Continued

Category	Method of Notification			
	From the Company Directly	Identified Suspicious Activity	Notified by Third Party/Bank	Heard Media Reports
Postgraduate	53%	12%	14%	36%[1,2]
Race/ethnicity				
Non-Hispanic white	56%[4]	10%	14%	30%[3]
Non-Hispanic black	56%	5%	26%	33%
Hispanic/ Latino	62%[4]	7%	22%	19%[1]
Non-Hispanic other	40%[1,3]	28%[+]	17%	29%
Comfort level with modern technology				
Very	55%[3,4]	10%[4]	16%	30%[3,4]
Moderately	53%[3,4]	10%[4]	18%	31%[3,4]
Somewhat	73%[1,2]	9%	13%	16%[+]
Not at all	77%[1,2]	3%[1,2]	18%	3%[+]

NOTE: [+] denotes statistically significant differences from all other groups within a demographic category. [1, 2, 3, or 4] denotes statistically significant differences from the noted group, within a demographic category. Significance was calculated at $p < 0.05$ for all noted differences using the Wald test.

The 11 percent of consumers who stopped dealing with the company combined with the 23 percent who do less business with the company than before (as shown in Figure 2.5) resulted in 34 percent of consumers who received a data breach notification.

Figure B.1
Did You Stop Dealing with or Do Less Business with the Firm Following the Breach (of Those Who Had Ever Received a Notification in Their Lifetime, n = 998)?

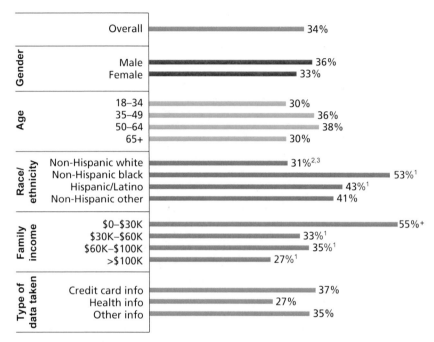

	Overall	34%
Gender	Male	36%
	Female	33%
Age	18–34	30%
	35–49	36%
	50–64	38%
	65+	30%
Race/ ethnicity	Non-Hispanic white	31%[2,3]
	Non-Hispanic black	53%[1]
	Hispanic/Latino	43%[1]
	Non-Hispanic other	41%
Family income	$0–$30K	55%+
	$30K–$60K	33%[1]
	$60K–$100K	35%[1]
	>$100K	27%[1]
Type of data taken	Credit card info	37%
	Health info	27%
	Other info	35%

NOTE: + denotes statistically significant differences from all other groups within a demographic category. [1,2,3,] or [4] denotes statistically significant differences from the noted group, within a demographic category. Significance was calculated at $p < 0.05$ for all noted differences using the Wald test.

RAND *RR1187-B.1*

Figure B.2
Percentage of Participants Who Recalled Receiving a Breach Notification in the 12 Months Preceding the Survey (Percentage of Those Who Recalled Ever Receiving a Breach Notification in Their Lifetime, n = 998)

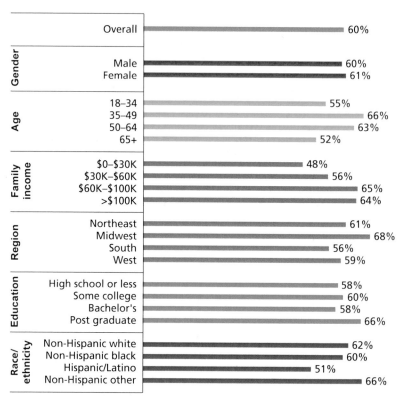

Table B.3
Demographic Tabulation of Survey Respondents (n = 2,038)

Group	Count	Percentage
Gender		
Male	948	47%
Female	1,090	53%
Age		
18–34	355	17%
35–49	596	29%
50–64	738	36%
65+	349	17%
Family Income		
$0–$30K	520	26%
$30K–$60K	535	26%
$60K–$100K	495	24%
>$100K	480	24%
Missing	8	0%
Region		
Northeast	362	18%
Midwest	374	18%
South	700	34%
West	602	30%
Education		
High school or less	370	18%
Some college	744	37%
Bachelor's	530	26%
Postgraduate	394	19%
Race/ethnicity		
Non-Hispanic white	1,367	67%
Non-Hispanic black	233	11%
Hispanic/Latino	326	16%
Non-Hispanic other	112	6%

NOTE: Percentage totals might not sum to 100 due to rounding.

References

114th Congress, 1st Session, Data Security and Breach Notification Act of 2015, Senate Bill 177, January 13, 2015a. As of February 5, 2016: https://www.congress.gov/bill/114th-congress/senate-bill/177/text

114th Congress, 1st Session, Data Security Act of 2015, House of Representatives Bill 2205, May 1, 2015b. As of February 5, 2016: https://www.congress.gov/bill/114th-congress/house-bill/2205/text

Ablon, Lillian, Martin C. Libicki, and Andrea A. Golay, *Markets for Cybercrime Tools and Stolen Data: Hackers' Bazaar*, Santa Monica, Calif.: RAND Corporation, RR-610-JNI, 2014. As of February 19, 2016: http://www.rand.org/pubs/research_reports/RR610.html

"Amid Rampant Data Theft, Consumers Left Breached and Burned Out," *The Security Ledger*, May 4, 2015. As of February 9, 2016: https://securityledger.com/2015/05/amid-rampant-data-theft-consumers-left-breached-and-burned-out/

Anderson, Keith B., *Identity Theft: Does Risk Vary with Demographics?* Washington, D.C.: Federal Trade Commission, Bureau of Economics, Working Paper 279, August 2005.

BakerHostetler, "Data Breach Notification Laws," *Data Privacy Monitor*, undated. As of February 9, 2016: http://www.dataprivacymonitor.com/category/data-breach-notification-laws/

Beshears, J., J. J. Choi, D. Laibson, and B. C. Madrian, "How Does Simplified Disclosure Affect Individuals' Mutual Fund Choices?" in David A. Wise, ed., *Explorations in the Economics of Aging*, Chicago: University of Chicago Press, 2011, pp. 75–96.

Brandeis, Louis D., *Other People's Money and How the Bankers Use It*, New York: Frederick A. Stokes Company, 1914.

Cárdenas, Alvaro A., Svetlana Radosavac, Jens Grossklags, John Chuang, and Chris Jay Hoofnagle, "An Economic Map of Cybercrime," TPRC, August 15, 2009. As of February 5, 2016:
http://ssrn.com/abstract=1997795

"Changes to California's Data Breach Notification Requirements," *National Law Review*, October 22, 2015. As of February 9, 2016:
http://www.natlawreview.com/article/
changes-to-california-s-data-breach-notification-requirements

Conn, Joseph, "Blues Plans Will Offer Free, Perpetual Credit and Fraud Protection," *Modern Healthcare*, July 15, 2015. As of February 9, 2016:
http://www.modernhealthcare.com/article/20150715/NEWS/150719950

Consumer Financial Protection Bureau, "Testing 'Know Before You Owe' Mortgage Forms: Qualitative and Quantitative Tests Show New Forms Improve Consumer Understanding, Aid Comparison Shopping, and Help Prevent Surprises," fact sheet, November 20, 2013. As of March 6, 2015:
http://files.consumerfinance.gov/f/201311_cfpb_factsheet_kbyo_testing.pdf

Garrison, L., M. Hastak, J. M. Hogarth, S. Kleimann, and A. S. Levy, "Designing Evidence-Based Disclosures: A Case Study of Financial Privacy Notices," *Journal of Consumer Affairs*, Vol. 46, No. 2, 2012, pp. 204–234.

Government Accountability Office, *Data Breaches Are Frequent, but Evidence of Resulting Identity Theft Is Limited; However, the Full Extent Is Unknown*, Washington, D.C., GAO-07-737, 2007.

Groves, Robert, *Survey Errors and Survey Costs*, New York: John Wiley and Sons, 1989.

Halzack, Sarah, "Home Depot and JPMorgan Are Doing Fine. Is It a Sign We're Numb to Data Breaches?" *Washington Post*, October 6, 2014. As of September 18, 2015:
http://www.washingtonpost.com/news/get-there/wp/2014/10/06/
home-depot-and-jpmorgan-are-doing-fine-is-it-a-sign-were-numb-to-data-breaches/

Harrell, Erika, *Victims of Identity Theft, 2014*, Bureau of Justice Statistics, NCJ 248991, 2015.

Harrell, Erika, and Lynn Langton, *Victims of Identity Theft, 2012*, Bureau of Justice Statistics, NCJ 243779, 2013.

Herr, Trey, and Sasha Romanosky, "Cyber Crime: Security Under Scarce Resources," American Foreign Policy Council Defense Technology Program Brief, No. 11, June 24, 2015.

Hoch, Stephen J., and George F. Loewenstein, "Time-Inconsistent Preferences and Consumer Self-Control," *Journal of Consumer Research*, Vol. 17, 1991, pp. 492–507.

Hoofnagle, Chris Jay, and Jennifer King, "What Californians Understand About Privacy Online," 2008.

Hu, Elise, "I Feel Nothing: The Home Depot Hack and Data Breach Fatigue," *NPR*, September 3, 2014. As of September 18, 2015: http://www.npr.org/sections/alltechconsidered/2014/09/03/345539074/i-feel-nothing-the-home-depot-hack-and-data-breach-fatigue

Javelin Strategy and Research, *2011 Identity Fraud Survey Report: Consumer Version*, Pleasanton, Calif., February 2011.

Levin, Adam, "How This Federal Data Breach Law Could Actually Hurt Consumers," *Forbes*, March 27, 2015. As of August 14, 2015: http://www.forbes.com/sites/adamlevin/2015/03/27/how-this-federal-data-breach-law-could-actually-hurt-consumers

Libicki, Martin C., Lillian Ablon, and Tim Webb, *The Defender's Dilemma: Charting a Course Toward Cybersecurity*, Santa Monica, Calif.: RAND Corporation, RR-1024-JNI, 2015. As of February 8, 2016: http://www.rand.org/pubs/research_reports/RR1024.html

Loewenstein, George, Leslie John, and Kevin Volpp, "Using Decision Errors to Help People Help Themselves," in Eldar Shafir, ed., *The Behavioral Foundations of Public Policy*, Princeton, N.J.: Princeton University Press, 2012, pp. 361–379.

Madden, Mary, and Lee Rainie, *Americans' Attitudes About Privacy, Security and Surveillance*, Washington, D.C.: Pew Research Center, May 20, 2015. As of February 8, 2016: http://www.pewinternet.org/2015/05/20/americans-attitudes-about-privacy-security-and-surveillance/

Microsoft Corporate Blogs, "#MSFTCOSO POV: Millennials, Baby Boomers, Technology and the Internet: New Data," *Microsoft of the Issues*, November 3, 2014. As of February 8, 2016: http://blogs.microsoft.com/on-the-issues/2014/11/03/msftcoso-pov-millennials-baby-boomers-technology-internet-new-data/

National Conference of State Legislatures, "Security Breach Notification Laws," January 4, 2016. As of February 8, 2016: http://www.ncsl.org/research/telecommunications-and-information-technology/security-breach-notification-laws.aspx

NetDiligence, *Cyber Claims Study*, 2014. As of February 8, 2016: http://www.netdiligence.com/NetDiligence_2014CyberClaimsStudy.pdf

Newcombe, Tod, "States Approach Federal Data Breach Law with Caution," *Governing*, October 2014. As of August 14, 2015: http://www.governing.com/columns/tech-talk/gov-federal-cybersecurity-law.html

Office of the Press Secretary, "Fact Sheet: Safeguarding American Consumers and Families," White House, January 12, 2015. As of February 8, 2016: https://www.whitehouse.gov/the-press-office/2015/01/12/fact-sheet-safeguarding-american-consumers-families

Perlberg, Steven, "Do Consumers Have Data Breach Fatigue?" *Wall Street Journal*, October 9, 2014. As of September 18, 2015:
http://blogs.wsj.com/cmo/2014/10/09/data-breach-impact-yougov/

Ponemon Institute, *The Aftermath of a Data Breach: Consumer Sentiment*, April 2014. As of February 8, 2016:
http://www.ponemon.org/local/upload/file/
Consumer%20Study%20on%20Aftermath%20of%20a%20Breach%20
FINAL%202.pdf

———, *2014: A Year of Mega Breaches*, January 2015. As of February 8, 2016:
http://www.ponemon.org/local/upload/file/
2014%20The%20Year%20of%20the%20Mega%20Breach%20FINAL_3.pdf

RAND American Life Panel, "Panel Weighting," undated. As of February 8, 2016:
https://alpdata.rand.org/index.php?page=weights

Romanosky, S., and A. Acquisti, "Privacy Costs and Personal Data Protection: Economic and Legal Perspectives of Ex Ante Regulation, Ex Post Liability and Information Disclosure," *Berkeley Technology Law Journal*, Vol. 24, No. 3, 2009.

Romanosky, S., D. Hoffman, and A. Acquisti, "Empirical Analysis of Data Breach Litigation," *Journal of Empirical Legal Studies*, Vol. 11, No. 1, 2014, pp. 74–104.

Romanosky, S., R. Telang, and A. Acquisti, "Do Data Breach Disclosure Laws Reduce Identity Theft?" *Journal of Policy Analysis and Management*, Vol. 30, No. 2, 2011, pp. 256–286.

Senate Rules Committee, State Senate of California, Personal Information: Privacy: Breach, Senate Bill 570, bill analysis, May 21, 2015. As of February 8, 2016:
http://www.leginfo.ca.gov/pub/15-16/bill/sen/
sb_0551-0600/sb_570_cfa_20150522_151612_sen_floor.html

Shey, Heidi, "Market Overview: Customer Data Breach Notification and Response Services," Forrester, August 5, 2015. As of February 5, 2016:
https://www.forrester.com/Market+Overview+Customer+Data+Breach+
Notification+And+Response+Services/fulltext/-/E-res121314

State Legislature of California, Medical Information, Assembly Bill No. 1755, September 18, 2014a. As of February 9, 2016:
http://www.leginfo.ca.gov/pub/13-14/bill/asm/ab_1751-1800/
ab_1755_bill_20140918_chaptered.pdf

———, Personal Information: Privacy, Assembly Bill No. 1710, September 30, 2014b. As of February 9, 2016:
http://leginfo.legislature.ca.gov/faces/
billNavClient.xhtml?bill_id=201320140AB1710

U.S. Census Bureau, "State and County QuickFacts," undated. As of February 9, 2016:
http://quickfacts.census.gov/qfd/states/00000.html

Verizon, *2014 Data Breach Investigations Report,* 2014.

Wash, Rick, and Emilee Rader, "Too Much Knowledge? Security Beliefs and Protective Behaviors Among United States Internet Users," *Symposium on Usable Privacy and Security,* 2015, pp. 309–325. As of February 8, 2016:
https://www.usenix.org/system/files/conference/soups2015/soups15-paper-wash.pdf

"World's Biggest Data Breaches," *informationisbeautiful,* undated. As of September 16, 2015:
http://www.informationisbeautiful.net/visualizations/
worlds-biggest-data-breaches-hacks/

Zickuhr, Katherine, *Generations and Their Gadgets,* Washington, D.C.: Pew Research Center, February 3, 2011. As of February 8, 2016:
http://www.pewinternet.org/2011/02/03/generations-and-their-gadgets/